BLACK BELT LIBRARIANS

Every Librarian's
Real World Guide
to a Safer Workplace

Warren Davis Graham, Jr.

PURE HEART PRESS
Main Street Rag Publishing Company
Charlotte, North Carolina

*The opinions expressed in this book are my own and
do not necessarily reflect those of any previous or
current employer of mine. But they should.*

Library of Congress Control Number: 2006903772

ISBN: 1-59948-027-1

Produced in the United States of America

Pure Heart Press
Main Street Rag Publishing Company
4416 Shea Lane
Charlotte, NC 28227
www.MainStreetRag.com

6013

For my co-workers on "Planet Library"; especially for the librarian who once left me this anonymous note before one of my presentations:

"Where in the library is the most appropriate place for crazy people to hang out?"

Contents

Acknowledgements

Thanks to my grandmother, Mary Flowers, who I often quote in my seminar. She was always there for me whenever I needed her with constant love. I miss her every day. She saved the child.

Thanks to my high school guidance counselor, William "Bill" Lindsay who took time to listen to a lost and petrified high school senior. He encouraged my college education and was the first adult to tell me I had potential. He saved the teenager.

And thanks to my wife Jessica, who is even more beautiful on the *inside*. I would not be writing this were it not for her encouragement. I couldn't accomplish much without her. She saved the man.

Introduction

The then Library Director, Robert Cannon, called me up one afternoon during my duties as Security Manager for an uptown mall that was situated right across the street from the main library. The library was closed temporarily, being refurbished and expanded from 60,000 to 160,000 square feet. He asked me how I went about controlling the many center city and potential problems in my facility. He then quickly stole me away. Two weeks later, I was working for the library, only one short month before its grand re-opening.

I quickly saw that we were going to have our hands full. The late Nina Lyon, one of the finest overall librarians I have ever known and the then manager of the main library building took me on a tour and laid out the situation. She told me that in the old building she had to handle multiple security situations every single day. There had been no formal rules for library use and no consistency in the attempts to control behavior. They had gone through several contract security companies that had all categorically failed. There was no standardized record keeping and most of the daily "patrons" were not using the building as a library, but as a home.

While a few of the staff thought we should never ban or deny access to anyone no matter what they did, I countered by saying that they *would* be denying access to the regular, true library user if they didn't control the environment and keep it conducive to library use. Yes, it is indeed a public building, but what type? Well, it's a bloody *library*, and it should look and feel like one. It's not a place for people to come in and do anything they want. Just because we are a "public building" doesn't mean you can build a camp fire in the middle of non-fiction.

We were successful in our security efforts thanks to my development of a solid, *simple* program and procedures. We involved all of the employees and trained them properly. We were more than fair in the advisement of rules and most importantly, from day one, we made sure that we treated *everyone* the same.

Let me state here that despite the success, I do not consider myself a security "expert," even though a lot of folks refer to me that way. Actually, I don't believe there is any such thing, and I will explain.

My reason is two fold. First, there is no way you can keep up with the physical security field, i.e. alarm systems, cameras, building access systems, and the like unless you actually work in that specific industry. Technology is growing so fast that new products are constantly being produced and the security products that are available to you today are really already dated.

Secondly, no two security situations are quite alike. Human interaction is always dynamic and never static. It's always in flux. Rarely is there a *black and white* solution to an incident; it's almost always *grey*. Even though I've been doing this for quite a while, I still make mistakes and find challenges in ascertaining what is really going on and picking the best response I can. I can still certainly be taken aback by the mental state of some of our "reality impaired" patrons. Some days I feel as though all I do is try to keep the patients calm!

The one advantage that I do have in my attempts to help you over most others in the security field is that I do indeed work on the front line in a library. Within the library system in Charlotte there are a total of 24 libraries and they are of all shapes and sizes in all types of areas. Their staffing varies from very large to others that at times have a single librarian minding the store. In most cases, the library staff also wear the security hats along with their other duties. The point I am trying to make here is that I know exactly what a librarian goes through. I witness it first hand everyday.

I wish I could have had the information that I am going to share with you when I first started working with the public when I was very young. Even though I would deal with the public for ten years in retail before I stumbled into the security field, many of the principles I work by today would have readily applied, and I would now have more hair.

As you may have guessed from the title of the book, I will speak of how martial art has influenced my perspective in interacting with the problem patron. Don't jump to the conclusion that I am talking about *physical* encounters and that my mentioning of my experience in martial ways implies that I think I am some sort of tough guy. It's the *mental* aspect of that discipline that I want you to consider, as you will see.

I'm going to share with you the basis of everything I know about dealing with all levels and all kinds of people in various security situations. You will find that I am rather straight forward and down right blunt at times. I call this, after all, a "real world" guide. I prefer to tell it to you the way it really is versus what you may want to hear. I relate the stories as they happened; colorful, earthy language and all. As I'm sure you can already tell, I'm certainly not a professional writer, so I hope you will bear that in mind. I hope the usefulness of the content makes up for my tortured syntax and overall punishment of the English language.

The information contained within is simple. There is a great strength in simplicity, but our oh, so magnificent intellect convinces us that the best solutions are the most complicated, and we sometimes end up out thinking ourselves. Einstein once said that when you can't find a solution to a problem, you need to go back to the basics! I'm reminded of that popular expression these days that tells everyone to "think outside the box," but that presupposes that one can think *inside* the box to start with!

However, *simple* does not always mean *easy*. These tactics that I'm providing you take practice, especially if you are passive by nature, which most (but certainly not all) librarians are. I don't mean that in a demeaning way. We are all born passive (as I was) or aggressive by our very nature and we tend to follow that genetic predisposition throughout our lives. I'm going to help you to be more assertive if you need to be.

I believe that you have to have a certain level of people skills to be able to keep your sanity when working with the public. Not all patrons are pleasant to deal with, but the bad patrons are still patrons nonetheless. Every day at the reference desk is not going to be full of moonlight and canoe rides. I am sorry that they failed to teach you in library school that all the nuts aren't in the nuthouse. Some of the librarians I've worked with don't even like the public and I have often wondered why in the world they ever became involved in a profession that demands helping people!

The whole idea, and my fervent wish in producing this text, is to empower you to be able to *respond* to a situation rather than simply *react*. Animals react, people should respond. However, since we humans are creatures of emotion and not logic, we often do something and then think about it rather than the opposite. I'm going to show you a way to put a plan of action in place, then you can take the first step in controlling your environment.

You are a professional librarian. You go the extra mile for the patrons and want them to get the information they are seeking. In turn, you only ask that they treat you in a civil manner and not abuse you. I think that is quite fair enough.

There have been a many a librarian that has corresponded with me after my presentation, testifying to the effectiveness of my little strategies. Trust me, being a passive, introverted, emotive soul that I tend to be; if I acquired these skills, anyone can.

Chapter One:

The Inmates Are Running the Asylum

Before we get too serious, I'll start on the lighter side at the request of so many of my seminar attendees over the years. I've included a few abbreviated tales from my tenure as a library security manager. While I could dedicate the entire book to such stories, I've just picked a few of the best. Of course they are all true. Who could make these up?

To begin with, some folks will try to tell you that there is no such thing as a dumb question. Obviously they never worked in a library. The top ten dumbest things I have been asked while standing by the circulation desk:

10) *"If it's a cloudy day, will they postpone the eclipse of the sun?"*

9) *"Do your elevators go upstairs?"*

8) *"Who was that Wells guy and how did he build that time machine?"*

7) *"Who didn't sign the Declaration of Independence?"*

6) *"Can I flex something in here?"* (They were actually looking for a fax machine)

5) "Do you have books on witchcraft? My ex-wife has put a mojo on me and now I can't have sex with my girlfriend and my trailer has been repossessed."

4) "Do you have an Orlando newspaper? They have a bunch of felony warrants out for me there and I want to see if I'm in the paper."

3) "How late can I use the computers after you close?"

2) "There's a sign out there that says "NO PARKING" in big letters. Can I park there?"

1) "Just where in the hell is uptown Charlotte and where is the damn library?"

During my first week at the library, a woman exited a taxi in front of the library. She said hello to everyone at the front desk and said she was leaving town, but wanted to do something for the library. She pulled out a checkbook and wrote us a check for one million dollars. After giving it to the stunned circulation staff, she got back in the taxi, never to be seen again. The check was phony, of course.

Another lady happily greeted me one morning as I opened the front door. She asked me where the closest copier was and I took her to it. She then proceeded to pull off her wig and make a copy of it. She thanked me for my help and left.

I once walked into the bathroom to find a fellow that was at least 6'6" tall standing nude in front of the sink and mirror. Nude, that is, with the exception of one sock, pulled up over his knee. He was busy lathering up his entire body, and he turned toward me with a fierce, confrontational look in his eyes. Knowing he probably had an issue or two, I wanted to approach him as easy as possible and decided to use a little humor. "Hey, my friend," I said smiling, "You've lost a sock haven't you?" pointing to his bare foot. He looked at me, down at his foot and then back to me. "Hell boy," he grumbled, "I just found this one!"

I was standing by the front entrance when a huge, boat-like '72 Buick screeched halfway up on to the sidewalk and slammed on brakes, almost hitting a prominent "No Parking" sign. The micro mini-skirted driver jumped out, leaving the engine running and ran past me and up to the typewriter room that we had at the time. The room was windowed, so I could clearly witness the woman pulling out a huge pile of blank business checks and typing frantically.

I called the police, and as I was waiting for them to arrive and check things out, I got a good look at the woman. *He* was over six feet tall and very slim. His black Tina Turner wig was askew on his head and his falsies were protruding above his knit top. I don't know where he got a pair of heels to fit his huge, narrow feet, but they must have been a size 18. The police arrived and arrested the fellow, who had just stolen the checks from a car uptown. To this day I have never seen another thief bring so much attention to himself.

One afternoon I was called to the non-fiction reading room to find a man face down on a table in a huge pool of gooey, dark burgundy liquid. The mess covered the 4'x6' table and dripped over the sides. My first reaction was that he had hemorrhaged somehow, someway, and that he was DRT (dead right there). The responding medics proved me in error. The man had actually guzzled a half gallon bottle of wine before coming in and was so drunk that he had thrown it all up as he passed out. The maintenance staff was very excited about having to replace 26 carpet squares.

I'll never forget the petite little lady that came out of the bathroom one morning. This was a young woman, probably in her 20's. On every inch of exposed skin, including her face and neck, she had hundreds of tiny, open and bleeding sores. I still have no idea what she was suffering from, but she was obviously very ill. She had taken toilet paper and had pressed it over the sores on her arms. I immediately asked her if she needed medic, trying to find out if she needed help. In 25 years of security work, I have never been cursed at like that. She called me everything, and I do mean everything. Luckily, she said all of it as she was walking out the door and I never saw her again.

I was once called to the ladies restroom by a patron who said something weird was happening in one of the stalls. I walked in and under the stall wall I saw four feet extremely closed together. I knocked on the door, and after some hesitation and rapid adjustment of clothing, a man and woman came sheepishly walking out. He explained that they were having an affair and that the library was the only place they could meet. She was married and he was an ex-felon on parole. She wailed not unlike someone at a Pentecostal funeral and begged me not to call her husband. He was literally on his knees, pleading with me to not call his parole officer. All this made for quite a scene.

Another memorable restroom moment was when I discovered a huge area of excrement on the floor of a stall, right in front of the toilet bowl. When I returned less than one minute later with a maintenance person, someone was sitting and using that very toilet! He had his legs spread to keep his feet out of the previously mentioned mess.

I was called to the reference area on 9-11-2001; just an hour or so after news broke of the tragedy at the World Trade Center. A 78 year old gentleman was fist fighting with a 68 year old over a business reference book. They were swinging in slow motion, but both obviously had bad intentions. One had already bitten a chunk out of the other's shoulder. I remember thinking that the whole world must be going crazy that day.

A fellow came slowly walking into the library one night. He was looking at the ceiling for the most part and he caught my attention. He then went by one of the service desks and just stood there, looking straight up. I decided to talk to him, but as I started to go over, he moved on to the elevators and went to the second floor. My instinct told me that I needed to go up and check him out.

I found him in the men's room, where he had taken six rolls of toilet paper and was proceeding to cram them in the commode with his foot. When I approached him, he stopped and turned and just looked at me. I escorted him to the security office and informed him that I was banning him. The entire time he never changed his blank, calm facial expression and never said a word. It was the first and last time I ever saw him.

A patron who had attempted to steal a couple of paperbacks and had, in a drunken stupor, assaulted one of the security staff, was detained in the security office. I was assisting the arresting police officer by going through the suspect's jacket, shirt and pants pockets. We found 14 various knives, box cutters and sharpened screwdrivers.

I literally saved a pervert from his victim one morning. He had exposed himself to her in the stacks and she really got upset. He actually came to me for help! I had more trouble keeping her away from him than I did actually banning him. "Go ahead!" he begged me. "Take my damn picture so I can get out of here!"

The second top 10 dumbest things that were asked of me or the staff:

10) *"Is it true there are Jewish people in the Bible?"*

9) *"Why are the letters of the alphabet in that particular order?"*

8) *"Can you give me the address of the local church of Satan?"*

7) *"Where are they holding Elvis and where can I write him?"*

6) *"Can I rent a shower here?"*

5) *"Why doesn't ex-president Kennedy ever speak out like Clinton does?"*

4) *"My name is Satan Leviathan Beelzebub. Ever heard of me?"*

3) *"Where did they really film that Armstrong on the moon crap?"*

2) *"If my parents were both Italian, does that make me Italian?"*

1) *"Where did Lee Harvey Oswald shoot John Wilkes Booth?"*

Chapter Two:

Entering the Ring: Essential Elements of an Effective Program

In my experiences both with the public library in Charlotte and during my consulting travels, I have often seen the same repeated issues. In my opinion, these are the main points you must take into consideration if you're going to have a truly effective security and safety program. These are the fundamentals. Leave out any of these and your procedures will be lacking.

1. You must have established rules and regulations for library use. While *most* rules in libraries I have seen are for the *most* part common sense, as Voltaire put it best, "Common sense is not so common."

The rules have to be clear and concise so you can interpret them with confidence in the midst of a security incident. When everything is hitting the fan, you have no time to dig through some nebulous policy, trying to figure out if a rule applies to the situation and to what extent.

A critical point: Administration has to know what they want to accomplish with the security program, and you need to know that they are going to back you up once you advise someone of policy. Everyone has to be on the same page. You simply cannot have priorities that administration doesn't have, and they cannot expect you to follow procedures if they overturn your front-line decision each time a patron complains to them.

When you develop the rules for your library it then has to be established who will advise the patron of those rules. Can a part-time page tell a patron they can't have food and drink in the library, or must they always report rule infractions to a full time employee? Or you do only allow managers to advise patrons of rules? If you have security, at what point do they step in?

2. Vow never to say these five things again, because they mean   absolutely nothing and can put you in harm's way sooner or later:

A. *"He's harmless."* Very few human beings are completely harmless under the right circumstances.

B. *"He has never been a problem before."* The news is full of first time criminals.

C. *"We have never had a problem before."* Maybe (and probably), you've just been lucky. If there is one village idiot, he *will* find his way to the library sooner or later.

D. *"We have always done it that way."* That doesn't mean you are doing it right.

E. *"Other libraries do it that way."* That doesn't mean they know what is best for you (or even for them for that matter). Think for yourselves.

3. When advising patrons of rules you must always go by their *behavior* and never their *appearance.* You must have the same consequences for everyone no matter what their station in life *appears* to be. Also, I refer to all the folks I have to deal with as "behavior problems." We never call them anything that could make us sound biased in any way, so please forget terms like "Street People," "Yuppies from Hell" or "Satan's Spawn"!

4. You have to be consistent in enforcement. Once you set the new standard you have to stay on top of it each day. Who is going to be banned and for how long? Who is detained for arrest and how? Who is prosecuted and for what offenses? All things to consider before you start a new program.

5. You must control your environment through your constant awareness. Awareness is *the* key element to protecting yourself anywhere you are, and that certainly includes the workplace. Practice cultivating your awareness of what is going on around you and soon it will become second nature. You can do this without becoming paranoid and in a short time you develop a kind of sixth sense.

During my retail years I could tell you immediately when a potential shoplifter came in the store. Similarly, the bad guy has also developed a sense of when someone has recognized that he may have bad intentions. He wants to go about his "business" in stealth and your awareness may be all it takes to dissuade him.

6. Document all security incidents. This is absolutely essential not only for administration, but for possible future reference. If, for instance, you ban someone and they someday return, you will not be able to have them arrested or prosecute them for trespassing if you cannot show the precise who, when and why of the ban.

You may also need to document every time you correct patron behavior to show how busy you are in your security endeavors. We all know that the day is long gone when we can go to administration, and say, *"Gee, we sure are busy down front and we have to talk to people all day about the rules"* and expect to get the help you need.

You can also record and keep track of your potential problems, including those patrons that may be establishing some pattern of wrongful behavior, as well as that guy that always seems to be staring at you and giving you the creeps. By documenting, you will have all the information you need for banning if that is what their behavior leads to. I have a form to help you with this in Chapter Eight.

7. You must establish a system to train all employees. You don't go into a lion cage with a book on lion taming. Everyone needs to know security and safety procedures up front, what is expected of them and *that they will be held accountable when they do not follow through.* They need to understand that security is

part of everyone's job and that one person not doing their part can collapse all the safeguards that have been put in place. *"Hey, I thought that you locked the front door last night before we left!"*

Training classes can be based on any number of things. You need a basic orientation for your new staff members and you need a review class everyone must attend annually. You should always incorporate security as part of any monthly or bi-monthly meetings you have with staff.

You can use role-playing or "synthetic training" sessions, which I think are some of the very best ways for everyone to get into the rhythm of patron interaction. Perform the exercises when the building is closed so you can actually execute in various areas where problems might occur, like the circulation desk. You need to make it as real as possible. This technique makes a huge difference over just training in a meeting room.

All staff take turns being bad guys and good guys, and you just set up an assortment of scenarios based on things that have actually happened. After a little initial nervousness, the passive staff members will see how much better they are than they expected, and they will be amazed at how some of the more aggressive folks flub everything up, which will give them even more confidence. Just be careful not to put two employees together who don't especially care for each other!

Here are some scenarios you could use:

What would you do if...

—A patron slammed his hand on the counter and said, *"I'm sick and tired of the library's poor service!"*

—Someone was asleep on a newspaper that a patron needed to use.

—A patron had his shirt off and was bathing in the bathroom.

—A patron cursed at you then immediately said, *"I'm so sorry. I've had a terrible week! If one more thing goes wrong! Please forgive me!"*

—After you corrected a teenager he said, *"Go shelve a book you stupid librarian!"*

—A student came up to you and said, *"I can't study over there. That women who came to sit at my table stinks like hell!"*

—A very upset patron told you, *"I can't even use this library. That guy keeps trying to talk to me and no matter how many times I tell him I'm trying to read, he keeps bothering me!"*

You can see all the areas you can explore. Plan this type of training after you share the information in Chapter Five and you will be surprised at how much staff will enjoy it and how much everyone gains.

And while we are on the subject of employees (librarians and later security), I would like to add that you should hire front line personnel that like people and that are not afraid of social interaction.

How can you work with the public if you don't like them and/or are scared to death of them?

You also have to have personnel of character so they will do what they need to when you are not around. Consistency in a security matter is vital. And please realize that they must have a good dose of common sense and discretion.

Give me someone with those essentials and I can teach them the skills they need, but if they don't innately have those three elements, I think you'll end up dropping your bucket down a dry well.

8. You must establish a key control system. If you can't tell me who has ever had a key of some type to your building and the current disposition of it, you need to re-key your building. Period.

This is not nearly as complicated as it may seem and it doesn't have to be expensive. That is, if you know what you want and how to plan it, instead of relying on most locksmiths, who make more money the more keys they sell you.

It breaks down like this: You will have master, area master and individual door keys. If you have a page that only needs access to the book drop area, they have that one door (or bin) key. They need in the employee entrance? Fine, they get a key to that one door as well. The idea is that precious few have a master to every area in the building. Your children's staff all need to have access to every door in that specific area? Then you can issue an area master to each of them.

Letter and number the keys by having the locksmith stamp them "M" for master, "AM" for area master and "D" for door. If you have five master keys made, stamp them "M-1," "M-2," "M-3," etc. The children's area master can be stamped "AM-1-#1," AM-1-#2," "AM-1-#3" and so on. Let's say you have a genealogical section that needs an area master. Stamp that one as "AM-2-#1." Your circulation area would be "AM-3-#1." For individual door keys you mark them the using the same method.

Place the first key in your locked key box that you will have installed in the manager's office. Only the manager and the assistant have access. Repeat after me, please. Only the manager and the assistant have access. If everyone can get into the key box, you will soon have keys lost or mishandled, and no one will want to admit to it. If someone loses keys, they pay at least $10 per key and you may want to consider a higher cost for losing master keys.

Simply make up a list of your numbered keys on your computer, the dates they were issued and who obtained them.

9. You must periodically review your procedures because your vulnerabilities change. The bad guys can, and often do, find ways to circumvent your security procedures. At least annually, management should sit down and take a hard, honest look at existing procedures, and determine how they need to be updated and improved.

10. You need to develop a security checklist to be used by all your branches on a monthly basis. You can include things such as:

— First aide kit stocked
— Outside lights all working
— Extra keys secured and accounted for

—New staff has received security training
—Snow melt in good condition
—Emergency numbers updated
—Fire extinguishers charged
—Emergency exits clear

You see what I mean. Include any items or areas that pertain specifically to safety and security. This monthly review is vital no matter what the size of your building or the level of your problems. It ensures safety procedures are on a level equal to any other statistics or procedure you follow.

11. You must have employee accountability and there must be consequences if proper safety procedures and guidelines are not followed. This is absolutely critical and something I find missing most often.

12. You need to develop a simple emergency plan for your building in case of fire, severe weather or a bomb threat. How do you evacuate the building and where does everyone meet outside? How do you notify the fire department? Who notifies the patrons and how do you sweep the building? If you have a monitored fire system and paging capabilities it makes things easier, but most libraries don't.

Where will you gather inside if you have a tornado warning? Do you have a weather radio to monitor conditions? Meet with your local fire department and have them come to your library to help you.

And finally a few words on hiring your own security personnel if you ever consider it or have them now. Whether they are actual library employees (which I would highly recommend) or you have a contract company employed (which usually doesn't work), these are the basics you need to consider.

1. You must have the right people carrying badges around your building and talking with your patrons, and I will be the first to tell you that they are not easy to find. They have to like people (patrons *and* staff) and get a sense of efficacy when they help. They should never think of anyone asking them for assistance as a nuisance or bother.

2. They have to be mature. You cannot have some Lash Larue strutting around with his spurs jingling and jangling thinking that he must "out tough" everyone to get them to comply. That type of security will get you into trouble very quickly. They must be confident and secure with themselves.

3. They must have decent level of fitness and need to look as though they could handle a physical situation if needed. This attribute in and of itself can deter a possible incident. Unfortunately, most people I see in security uniforms look as though they would have a cardiac infarction if they had to run 20 feet.

4. They have to stay off their butts most of the time and be both visible and vigilant. I can put anyone in a chair with a coffee and newspaper, but I want an "officer" and not a "guard." I want the officer moving around and observing the possible bad guys before they see the officer.

5. Don't dress your security officers in typical garb, i.e. the military type shirt with epaulets, the patches,

the silver name tag and clip on tie. They will look like a typical "guard" and experienced behavior problems know that most guards are ill-trained, have little authority and usually don't know what they are doing.

6. Make sure they can express themselves in written form as well as verbally. Reports can become court documents and need to be written in a professional manner. During the interview process, have them write out a description of the most difficult incident they have ever handled and see for yourself how they do. This is very important skill that they must have. There is a big difference between, "Let's eat grandma" and "Let's eat, grandma!"

In closing, I would again remind you to be honest in your assessment of your building needs. Hoping problems will go away by ignoring them or wishing you'll never have them is not the path to take. Be pro-active and make whatever changes you can. Get several staff members together and give them the assignment of thinking like a group of bad guys. Have them go over your building inside and out, and task them to discover the vulnerable areas. You don't need a fancy form, just a few sheets of paper. You may be surprised to see what they find.

Chapter Three:
Three Aces to Keep up Your Sleeve

I keep a little sign in my office near the door so I *have* to look at it every time I exit my office. I just printed it on my computer and all it says is "A.A.A." There are no fancy borders and it's not on any parchment or colored paper. It's not there to impress or to look good. It's my reminder that Warren needs to keep his head on straight today at work. A simple reminder of something that is hard to accomplish at times.

When you deal with an upset patron, the last thing you want is to make the situation worse by your own actions. That occurs a great deal more than some care to think about. We've all worked with someone who never will admit when they are wrong and it can be maddening. But how often do we take a real look at our own behavior and have the courage to see the error in our own ways?

Some of us have a more natural ability to be happy, content and confident than others. Nothing seems to bother some folks and they maintain a pleasant countenance. They are human like the rest of us, but are blessed with an even and positive temperament.

But most of us are just not that way. We tend to be a little more mercurial in our conduct. We go through cyclical highs and lows to varying degrees. I blame it on whoever came up with that damn yin/yang thing (yes, that's a joke). We have a bad day and it usually shows. How can you go about not letting one problem create another? The answer is that you must have an effective self-support system of some type and to do that, you have to know what really makes you tick. How can you have a positive effect on the patron if you can't have one on yourself?

You have to be aware of your shortcomings and this takes a lot of introspection. After all, you can't get a hold of yourself until you know what to grab on to! Understanding your emotions is a journey that ultimately only you can take. If I could simply tell you how, I'd be very rich indeed.

So, back to my little A.A.A. sign, which is such an important part of *my* self-support system. It stands for Attitude, Approach and Analysis.

Attitude:

Simply put, what is your frame of mind as you enter your work place? Are you having a good day or a bad one? What personal problems are eating at you? Car trouble? Family illness? Did the dog ruin the carpet last night? Or are you having work related problems? Do you want to make your boss disappear? Is your co-worker sending you to an early grave? Still fuming about that last work review? Or maybe you just don't feel like being at work today. There are quite a few mornings when I would simply like to stay in bed!

There are many things that can be troubling us. We all carry burdens. The trick is to develop ways to put them on a back burner while you are at work. Personnel manuals universally demand we not bring personal problems or feelings to the workplace. I'd like to ask the author of such instruction if I can visit them sometime in "Never, Never Land."

Emotions often guide us more than we care to admit and it's surprising how many are completely unaware of their overall affect. As I mentioned in the introduction, emotional thinking is the main reason we tend to *react* rather than *respond.* If you are an emotional based person (as I tend to be), rather than logic based, you had better learn to put your personal feelings aside and concentrate on the issue at hand, or you will never operate in an optimal fashion.

Early on in my martial arts experience, I found that it was easier to control another person compared to controlling myself. My instructor would talk of "mizo no kokoro" or a "mind like water." You had to keep your mind calm and focused, he said, like a calm body of water, to accurately reflect the world around you. Negative emotions were like ripples in the water, distorting the reflection. It's such a sweet little analogy, but it's so very difficult some days.

Another thing to consider is if you are passive or aggressive by nature. If you tend to be passive, you may have to find a way to be more assertive during certain security situations. Conversely, if you are naturally assertive, you may need to curb your tendency so not to make whatever is going on worse in some way.

Bryon wrote that "adversity is the first path to truth." If you do not have a handle on your emotions, personal prejudices (everyone has some prejudice against something on some level) and problems, they *will* surface during tense inter-personal situations! Make sure that if things do go south when you're attempting to communicate with a difficult patron, it's not your fault.

Approach:

What is the best way to approach *this* particular situation right now? How can I de-escalate the situation instead of making it worse? Remember what I said earlier about solutions often not being simply in black and white, but many times grey. Interactions with the public often demand much discretion. Contrary to popular belief, employees *are* paid to think. If your attitude is straight and your head clear you can come up with a reasonable course of action.

I'll give you an example. Let's say a man comes to the circulation desk, tosses some DVD's on the counter, smiles as he leans towards you and slurs, "Check these out for me, honey." His breath parts your hair. His eyes look like two tomatoes in a glass of buttermilk. Yes, he is blasted.

Your security procedures may call for you to call the police or security if you encounter someone who is intoxicated. But what would you do now? Would you call for help or would you check out the materials and get him out the door? See my point?

Analysis:

After an incident, it is paramount that you ask, both of yourself and your staff, what tactics worked and which ones failed. What could you have done differently to affect the outcome?

If you thought the attitude and approach were challenging, you haven't seen anything until you get employees in a meeting analyzing a security incident and trying to get anyone to admit they blew it. Most employees hate to admit when they are wrong and get a little uptight and defensive. Often they will sit and struggle to rationalize their actions away, putting more stress on themselves than if they just said they could have handled it better. Try to put them at ease. You'll have to show that you're doing this to help them. The purpose is not to criticize, but to work through the incident as a team.

Of course you not only want to revisit things when they go wrong, but when they go smoothly as well. Share the successful tactics with the staff not present at the time of the incident. The bottom line is to learn from everyone's mistakes as well as triumphs. Sooner or later, everyone has to deal with a behavior problem. Ultimately you are doing all of this for a safer workplace and greater peace of mind.

Exploring and working earnestly within these three areas will do much to improve your staff working together to make security incidents and their aftermath a great deal easier to live with.

Chapter Four:
The Tao of "No"

All right, here we go. Once you have all the elements worked out and you have a nice little list of rules that will help you control the conduct of your visitors, how in the world do you go up to a perfect stranger and tell them they can't be doing what they are doing? What do you say to most ensure their compliance?

One thing to keep in mind is that telling someone that they cannot do something is not synonymous with a "confrontation." If you feel that way when you approach someone, you are putting way too much stress upon yourself.

I have been telling folks "no" for quite a long time now. Here are some universal guidelines to help the process go smoothly for you. I use them every day:

1. Always approach patrons with the attitude that they will comply and that this not going to be a big deal. Most of your patrons will listen to you and correct their behavior if you walk up to them with

an easy manner. They either know better in the first place, are continuing with their behavior until someone tells them to stop, or they simply don't realize they are doing something wrong and will readily go along with you.

2. You can start off nice and then get more authoritative if you need too, but you can't do the opposite. If you come on too strong you can easily embarrass them into a confrontation, especially if they are with someone else or in a group. Even the look on your face can make a difference since you start communicating with your expression before you even open your mouth. So if you're having a bad day, take that frown off your mug before you walk up to a patron.

Two phrases I constantly use are, "I know you didn't know, but..." or "I know there isn't a (or you didn't see the) sign, but..." You are giving them an "out" and putting them at ease. The last thing you want them to think is that you think they are idiots (even though sometimes they are).

3. If you tend to gesticulate, always use palms up, openhanded gestures. Never point your finger at anyone and never, ever touch them. Remember to not get too close to them. Everyone has a comfort zone from which they like to communicate. Disturbed people are even more sensitive about their private space, so be careful and give everyone some distance.

4. Even though you should approach confidently, you also need to exercise a sense of due caution because, after all, you usually don't know the person.

Try to keep a table or a chair in between you; don't automatically go around and get beside them.

It's also very important to never turn your back on a patron whose behavior you've just corrected. I know of situations where the patron seemed to comply, then verbally, or at times physically, assaulted the employee when his back was turned. Keep the patron in your sight at least peripherally until you are a safe distance away. Remember that aggression is a survival instinct and there are many people out there that are waiting for just one more person to tell them "no."

I want to impress upon you how absolutely deceiving appearances can be. They are no reflection on how someone is going to react to you. Some of the toughest, meanest, most destitute looking people have been the first to comply, while often the most professional appearing can catch you unaware and be the biggest jerks.

5. If the patron appears to be under the influence of drugs or alcohol, call 911 or your security immediately.

6. As best you can, be deaf to insulting language directed at you (more on this later). Experienced behavior problems know that by upsetting you they can use your emotions against you and control you.

7. Never argue with a behavior problem. Most are quite experienced at pointless argument and you will seldom win. Many patrons have a PhD in "why," knowing that "why" can be an endless, open question. Some people on the street survive by talking, so don't get caught up in a no win situation.

Tell them what you can or can't do for them in a polite, clear, concise and direct way, and move on.

8. Be prepared to be accused of some type of prejudice. They'll sometimes say that you're just doing this to them because of their race, their age, their monetary status or lack thereof, the part of the country they are from; I've heard them all. One lady told me I was banning her because she was a Christian, like I would know that!

They may be accusing you of being biased because of past wrongs in their life, but most often they just want to put you on the defensive. Don't fall for this ploy and stay with the real issue at hand.

9. Remember that suspicion and actual guilt are two different things. When you approach patrons and you are not sure what is going on, give them the benefit of a doubt until you do. That's another reason why an easy and soft approach is so vital.

10. I'm always asked how to approach teens. Kids are kids and I don't care if the 14 year old kid is 6 ft. tall, he is still 14 and is thinking *like* a kid. I remember well that when I was that age I was frightened and unsure of myself. I was afraid of what might happen at home as well as at school. Those emotions simply had me acting in immature ways.

Today, I keep all that in mind as I go up to a group of teens that are being too loud or causing some other problem. Show them some respect and educate them to the purpose of the library. Give teens a little more leeway and an extra warning before you turn up the authority progressively if need be. I find that most teens are good kids and some of them just haven't had much guidance in their short lives.

11. And what about those moms and dads who let their children run through the building, climbing all over anything they can mount, and making life hell for your other patrons? I usually handle this in one of two ways. Out of thousands of similar situations, I can only remember two or three instances where the parent balked at me saying anything.

If the kid is doing something and is in imminent danger of getting hurt, I do approach him, but as easy as possible and in a way that shows nothing but my sincere concern for his safety. Let's say some tyke is climbing on that nice, abstract art sculpture that was donated to the library and sits by the circulation desk. Mom is busy checking out and is oblivious to her child's plight (something I unfortunately see quite often). I'll ease up and say in a soft voice something like, "Whoa hotshot....careful....I'm afraid you might fall."

I come on as low key as I can and avoid touching the child if at all possible. When mom turns in response, I always smile and try to *make sure she does not think I am implying that she is a bad parent.* That is the main thing you do *not* want to convey. Get the parent defensive, they get angry, and you get into an unpleasant encounter.

If I don't know where the parent is, I'll ask the kid where mom or dad is. If I don't get a response, I quickly get another staff member to come over so I am not alone with the child and then try to locate a parent.

If the child is not about to immediately hurl to his doom, but is well on his way, I'll locate the parent and say something like, "Excuse me sir, is that your little one over there?" If you come up easy and smile, there is very, very rarely a problem. The parent sees what the tyke is doing and goes to get them. Usually I get a sincere thank you and I close by making a comment that I see such energetic kids get away from folks all the time because they're excited to be in the library. Get what I'm saying to them? Good kid, good parent.

Add these pointers to your procedures and you will quickly see an improvement in patron compliance and employee confidence. You'll see how they blend in with the techniques in the next chapter. Now let's really get down to it.

Chapter Five:
Playing Chess With the Checker Player

My first security job was at a theme park on the border of North and South Carolina. I naturally wanted to do a good job and I wanted to please my boss. I wanted patrons to comply, but I didn't want to make them angry. I didn't want to be disliked by them. I also wanted to be safe and certainly not have to engage in a physical confrontation. In other words I wanted to do the best job I could and be an asset to the company. Does all this sound familiar?

When you entered the park, there were huge signs warning you that alcohol was not allowed anywhere on property. They turned out to be a lousy deterrent (we all know that patrons rarely read signs). There was many a good ol' boy who wasn't about to pay what he considered high prices for food inside the park. He would bring his own refreshments and proceed to drop the tailgate and have a family picnic right in the parking lot.

Now here came Warren in his huge patrol car, an '80 Malibu. It was my job to approach and inform these folks that they could give me their beer, wine, liquor or *moonshine* and stay, or they could keep it all and leave for the day. If they chose to keep the booze and leave, they did not get their admission fee back. As you might imagine, I learned a lot about approaching people and I learned it fast.

I was pretty successful and most folks, whether they liked it or not, complied, but I felt something was missing. Even though I was talking to a couple dozen patrons a day and many more on concert days, I didn't feel I had a good rhythm in my approach. I had created a few standard lines to apply, but really I was like a ship setting to sail without a crew. I had no real *strategy* and I was just not at the comfort level I wanted. Then I remembered a lesson that was taught me many years earlier which had nothing to do with security work. It made all the difference in raising my confidence level in these situations.

To help guide you along in this area, I have to share some personal history. Please stick with me as I explain how I developed my system for dealing with upset, irate or just plain disturbed patrons. This concept is where the idea for *Black Belt Librarians* originated.

During my early high school years, my grandfather overheard me talking about a bully that was torturing me on a daily basis. I was quite shy and had little self esteem or confidence in myself. My granddad knew of my interest in martial arts so he bought me my first book on the subject, which gave me the impetus to actually join a karate class. That action would change my life in countless ways.

Karate schools back in the day were few and far between and the ones that were around could be very intimidating. This one was certainly no different. At the tender age of 15, I was in my first Japanese Shotokan karate class and I was in for much more than I had expected!

Those first years in karate were brutal. My instructor taught the way he was taught by his Japanese instructor, which meant seeing just how badly you *really* wanted to be in class. It was a test of the spirit and will as much as it was how to physically throw a kick. We sparred with each other in class every night and this was before all the foam rubber padding that karate practitioners wear now. We were bare fisted and footed, and there were many teeth knocked out, collected and placed back in. Protective headgear, what was that? A classmate of mine broke another student's jaw in five places with a spinning kick. I once witnessed my instructor punch a fellow student smack in the nose one night just to see if he had the fortitude to come back to class. Our uniforms were speckled with blood and it was impressed upon us that they were little badges of honor.

It was all over the top by today's standards, but this was the Asian way to test your sincerity and character way back in 1969. My instructor constantly pushed our willingness to stick things out, which was the price we paid to learn from him. It was damn scary at times and it did not come easy for me, but I did not quit. And I am not telling you this to suggest how macho I am to have survived this, but to better make the point that I really want to impress upon you.

Now there was plenty of technical information taught about how to *physically* execute all the various punches and kicks, but nothing to help me with the *mental* side of things. There was no psychological *strategy* in the approach of my sparring partner and more importantly, no guidance on how to develop confidence in myself, and that is why I had started practicing in the first place! My instructor would yell, "Get tough, Graham! You've got to be brave!" or "Hit with confidence! Don't be afraid! Go get'em!" All this sounded good, but these were abstract terms. Either you had "confidence" and were naturally assertive or you weren't. The more I thought about not being afraid the more frightened I became.

I improved technically and eventually became a black belt, but I still really did not have true confidence in my abilities. *And how in the world can you optimally execute any type of action in your life if you don't honestly believe in yourself?*

I would continue to experiment with different styles of martial art and eventually stumbled upon an instructor that helped me the most where I actually needed it; from the neck up, inside my head. How little did I know that what he taught me would one day apply directly to my day-to-day duties as a security officer?

My new instructor taught me how to approach *different opponent types*. Fighting, he said, was 90% *mental*. It wasn't as much about being physically tough as it was developing skill in proper strategy. You just don't go in throwing punches, praying and hoping something connects, he pointed out. The informed martial artist alters his position according to the style of the fellow that's trying his best to knock his head off and out of the ring. Within days, this instructor had me feeling like I really knew what I was doing.

I couldn't control what my opponent was going to do, *but by concentrating solely on my strategy*, I didn't have time for any type of fear or apprehension. And the successful execution of my specific strategy, in turn, had a direct effect on limiting what my opponent could do against me, thus indirectly giving me the confidence I so needed. That worked then, I remembered, so could I adapt that idea to dealing with the public? Not in the physical way of course, but in a mental capacity.

I started making notes about the patrons I encountered at the park. Who was upset and to what varying degrees? In karate I had four major types of opponents and developed strategies to handle what they would try to do to me. Gradually, through much examination and experimentation in the field, I came up with four levels of emotion to watch for in a patron and developed strategies for them as well.

By concentrating on a specific strategy that is best for the patron's current level of emotion, you also avoid the pressure of what my instructor said were "peripheral opponents."

Let's say you are dealing with a patron who is upset about something and you're at the front desk. Often our minds start to go in all different directions. Instead of concentrating on the patron, analyzing his emotional level and responding with a specific strategy, we start worrying about various things. Our fears surface and start to confuse us. What if I say the wrong thing? What do my co-workers think about what I'm saying? The patron looks pretty mean. What if I can't handle this and he starts yelling at me? What will my boss think?

All of which have nothing to do with the task at hand. It's exactly like when I first started sparring. Instead of concentrating on my opponent, I was worried about what my girlfriend, family or instructor would think if I lost. And what if I was kicked and hurt? What if I wasn't in shape and ran out of gas? What if my opponent was too tough for me? Fear can be a bottomless pit.

So you step up to the patron that wants to talk to you. It's a beautiful day (hey, maybe it's even payday) and you've just had a great lunch, but now you are faced with a first rate, champion jerk. Here is what you must do:

1. You recognize that he is upset.

2. You ascertain in which level he is operating.

3. You *respond* with the strategy for that specific emotional state.

4. You concentrate and center on affecting your plan.

I use the acronym, "A.B.C.C." to remember these four emotional states. That stands for:

A. Anxiety

B. Belligerence

C. For "Control", as in *out* of control!

C. Calm

I put them in this alphabetical order because it's easy to remember, but these levels do not necessarily run in any order, so keep that in mind. I could try and impress you with fancier terms or a longer list, but there is no need, it's not my style and I am here to help you in the *real world*. This is what I use daily and it works for me so I know it will work for you. The simpler it is, the easier it is to retain under stress. Let's examine them one by one:

Anxiety:

You occasionally have patrons who are upset either about something real or imagined. They are in a state of "Anxiety," and agitated to some mild degree.

There can be a number of reasons why a patron is this way:

1. Of course, the most common is the stress the average person is under today. Time, money, commitments, all on a higher level than ever before, and it can wear anyone out. And we are living in an age of instant access, so folks tend to want what they are after *right bloody now*. Just think of how computer speed has changed in the past five years and how you can get irritated because your computer may

be slow on a given day even though it provides the knowledge of the world at your fingertips!

2. We are also over-stimulated. With so many news sources assaulting our senses with continuous, mostly negative, news via our computers, newspapers and television, it's no wonder many patrons can be on the edge.

3. Sometimes they come in defensive to start with. They have had a previous negative experience with the library or somewhere else so they step up to the desk a little edgy.

4. You can certainly be a victim of their bias before you even say anything to them. They don't like you because of your gender, race, profession, or Lord only knows what else. They don't give you a chance and you haven't even opened your mouth yet.

5. Occasionally you are the victim of what I call the "first 'no' phenomenon" when the patron doesn't believe you when you tell them you can't do what they want. They ask to speak to someone else to see if that person will tell them something can't be done just to make sure you know what you're talking about.

6. Sometimes they just don't understand what you are trying to tell them and they get frustrated and vent that towards you. Keep in mind that those D and F students we went to school with are still out there roaming the hills somewhere.

7. You will also have a patron sooner or later that just doesn't know how to express himself in any way but by being mean or nasty. My original boss Nina

Lyon and I used to have a laugh when she would remind me that, "Some people just aren't raised right." My grandmother would nudge me and observe that, "Some people are just mean as hell." You know, they were both right and that sums up some of the patrons I deal with as well as anything else I've heard or read.

8. And of course, some people that may darken your doorway are just "10-73" as the police put it. In other words, they are just crazy. They don't have signs around their neck to tell you so. Haven't you been engaged in conversations with patrons who want to discuss a problem and after several frustrating minutes it dawns on you that hey, it's not you, it's them! They don't exactly have both hands on the wheel.

The most important thing you can do when you recognize the state of "anxiety" is to stop what you are doing, look into their eyes and actively listen to them. That's what I said; stop, look and listen.

This is simple advice, but sometimes very hard to do when chaos reigns on your job. You have a line out the door, you're one employee short, so you can't take your lunch and your blood sugar is dropping. You're running out of change and now you can't find that damn book on hold that a patron has driven 30 miles for. But that is what you must do once you sense a state of anxiety in patrons. Stop what you are doing. Look at them. Listen to what they tell you. If you give them your undivided attention for just a couple of minutes, that's usually all it takes to get them back to the "calm" level where you want them. Even if they don't get what they want, at least they will probably be satisfied that someone honestly listened to them. And isn't that what everyone wants when they are upset?

The last thing you want to do is mimic the level of emotion the patron is in, which I saw happen once when a staff member reacted to a frustrated patron by saying, "Well if you think you have problems, just come around the desk and work with me for an hour!" No need to tell you what the patron did after she heard that.

Watch your body language and countenance; no crossed arms, hands on hips or frowning. Soften your speech and go a little lower than theirs, and they will focus in on what you are saying more. And of course, never forget the solid gold tactic of introducing yourself, getting their name and using it often during the conversation.

So hear them out and let them vent a little. We all get upset sometimes. Demonstrate a little honest empathy and that will usually neutralize any anger. And if the library was wrong (yes, sometimes the patron *is* right and they know *exactly* what they are talking about), apologize, promise to follow up and make sure you do so.

To give you an idea of the mood and pace you're attempting to set, here are some phrases you can use:

—*"We're here to help you and we're going to get this all worked out."* You're trying to make them feel at ease that you are interested in what they have to say.

—*"I understand what you're saying."* This is positive reinforcement that they are indeed being heard.

—*"If I don't have an answer for you, I'll find it."* Again sending the message of how intent you are in helping them as much as you can. And even though I say this, I rarely have to call in help since the patrons are usually satisfied I have sincerely done everything that I can for them.

— *"I need to ask some questions to make it easier for us to correct this."* At which point I pull out my ever present note pad, or grab a p—slip. This also lets them know you are listening and want to assist.

It is a result of your mishandling the patron during this stage of emotion that gets you complained about most often. Please remember that your recognition of their anxiety and your control of it by applying the proper strategy can keep things from getting much worse.

Belligerence:

In this stage the patron can begin really raising his voice or yelling. He may be cursing the library or the circumstances, but not *you* specifically. Other patrons can't help but hear and some may be startled.

This is the time where you *must* take a stand and establish your credibility with the patron immediately before things possibly get worse. This is critical and must be done quickly if you hope to gain control of the situation.

Some guidelines for what you could say:

— *"I'm ready to discuss this with you as long as it takes; I'm here to help you. But I'm not going to let you yell at me."*

— *"This is not helping us resolve things. Please settle down and we'll get it worked out."* Never tell anyone to "calm down". For some reason that is too cliché and it doesn't work as well.

—*"I need you to please lower your voice; I want to help you."*

—*"You've asked me, so please let me explain this to you."*

Please keep in mind that this is the worst time to ever lose your own temper, but I have seen this happen many times. "I'll have your job." "Oh yeah? Well, I get off work at five and I'll twist your head like a door knob!" Don't be emotional. Don't feel like you have to prove yourself or "one-up" the patron. Leave your wee little ego out of things. These patrons don't actually *know* you, so don't take their comments or actions personally.

Another important point is to keep eye contact with the patron as you talk to him. Does that prospect make you nervous? Use a little game of looking at his eyebrows or looking at one eye and then the other. This, for some reason I can't explain, alleviates some of the pressure you may feel when you need to stay face to face.

Learning to stand your ground with the patron can be more than a little intimidating at first, but the absolute worse thing you can do is to shrink away and let the patron rant on. He then often gets even more caught up in his own emotions. Once you communicate that his behavior is not going to be allowed, the patron will usually settle back to at least the "anxiety" stage.

Control, as in OUT *of Control:*

The third stage to discuss is one I hope you never see, but you probably will if you work with the public long enough. Now the patron has lost control and is cursing you specifically. They may be throwing things or damaging property. They may be communicating threats to you. They may even be drunk or high. This is the "out of control" stage of emotion. Now is the time to call your security or the police. The patron has checked out of the hotel reality and it is time to immediately take measures to protect yourself. Do not hesitate to call for help when things have deteriorated to this point.

You may be asking yourself if I expect you to pick up the phone and call for help in the face of someone threatening you. Yes, I do. I have found that if the patron is going to assault you, he has already made up his mind, somewhere deep down, to do so. You are far better off attempting to call for assistance. Even if you only get a chance to push 911 before he actually physically attacks you, help will be on its way.

Another reason this action is the smart play is that I have seen calling for help as a way of establishing your credibility with the patron. I have witnessed some extremely irate people come around quickly when they saw that the police were being called despite their best bullying display of emotion. You may also choose to take this action when they are in the "belligerence" stage if you think that, despite your best efforts, the "out of control" stage is imminent.

So now you have just handled a particularly challenging situation with a behavior problem and find yourself shaking like a leaf. Now what is going on, you ask. I was right, he was definitely wrong. I played him like Yo-Yo Ma plays Carnegie and I'm the one that's nervous? Why is this upsetting me so much?

Many a librarian has told me that they simply cannot handle confrontation of any kind. "I'm just not built that way," one of my co-workers recently opined to me. "You're a man, you're some type of karate guy and you're use to telling these people off. They will never listen to a woman or any librarian. And physically, I always feel like I'm just falling apart!"

Well, I am not going to let you off the hook so easy and for a good reason: *We all have the same initial and natural reaction to trouble.* I don't give a flip who you are and how much experience you have or lack thereof. In these situations, nature automatically takes over.

You have probably heard of the fight or flight reaction. The idea is that long ago our primitive ancestors with their tiny, undeveloped brains could only react one of two ways. Og, the caveman, goes over the hill and meets up with a very hungry saber toothed tiger. His little, limbic brain signals either to take off running back across the hill, or to stand and fight. That limbic system is still part of our brains today; it's sometimes referred to as our "emotional brain," among other things. It has no sense of time or logic and hasn't evolved. You could say it's still prehistoric. It is there to sense danger and make us react in time to save ourselves.

So what happens when this kicks in? Immediately your energy goes to your larger muscles to enable you to run faster or fight harder. Your fine motor skills go out the window. Thus, your hands shake and your knees quiver. Your adrenaline dumps and you become warm and flushed. You may get "butterflies" in your stomach.

Understand that you are *not* "falling apart." It is not raw fear you are experiencing. All this is nature's way of gearing you up for a confrontation and nothing more. If you didn't feel these things to some extent it wouldn't be natural.

Remember to breathe deeply as your shortened breath denies oxygen to your brain, thus hampering your thinking.

Understand these feelings for what they are and you will be able to deal with it better than you ever thought you could.

Calm:

The level of emotion you see most often is "Calm." Your patrons come in to get their materials, you have pleasant interaction and all is good with the world.

At times however, the patron may start off calm until you tell them about the $40 they owe in lost book charges. They usually go into any of the other stages quickly!

Be wary when the patron has been "out of control" and then becomes "calm." Be careful since he can flip back to out of control behavior like the flicking of a light switch. I witnessed a fellow throw a chair through a plate glass window then fall to his knees sobbing like a baby, apologizing and trying to write a check for the damage. Of course, the police had been notified and were on the way, but five minutes later and before they could get there he was trying to throw another chair!

So there you have it. My four strategies for any of the four levels of emotion that your patron/"opponent" may go through. They are all field tested and I use them everyday. As you practice and get your rhythm you'll see first hand that this has an extremely high success rate. While no strategy works all the time, you will find this will serve you well in the majority of situations.

But now we have to take a step back yet again to look at the toughest person you will really ever have to deal with. Do you remember? We touched on this individual earlier in a previous chapter when discussing "Attitude." The biggest adversary you will ever come up against is yourself. How will you handle your emotions? How will you recognize what is happening to you before it sabotages you? How do you stay in control? What do you say to the person in the mirror?

So what is the strategy for handling yourself? You can bet I had to develop one for Warren Graham, because I too am human and can be as vulnerable as anyone. I've come to know how my wee, little mind works and I know my demons. I work at being aware of the mechanics of my thoughts, especially when I am tired, over worked or stressed out. There is a many a day I have to kick myself very hard to get in the correct gear.

Chapter Six:
Ten Day-to-Day Staples of Security

As I travel around the country visiting libraries, I see the same problems over and over again. Here are some basic (and mandatory in my opinion) procedures for you to always be aware of that might make all the difference in keeping you and your co-workers safe.

1. Never, and I mean never, count money in view of patrons. Make up your deposits and balance the register or cash drawer before you open or after you close. Gone is the day you can run your library like Sam Drucker's general store in Hooterville (I'm really dating myself with that one). I've seen staff hurry in at *five minutes* before opening. They cut on the lights and maybe do a personal thing or two and open the doors to the public. *Then* they get out the cash and make sure it's counted properly; right in front of patrons. It looks like they're running some wheel of fortune game in Vegas. But that's ok, right? Because, after all, you've *never had a problem before* (remember Chapter Two).

You think you only open with, say, $50, so that doesn't offer a robber enough. Well, the bad guy doesn't know how much you have. All he sees is green. People are hurt for much less and $50 is a lot of money to a destitute person.

2. Whether you have money drawers or cash registers, make sure they stay locked when you are away from the circulation desk. Countless libraries are ripped off because there is no one at the desk and the drawer is not locked. If you are working up front and it's busy, it's ok to have it unlocked but *any other time*, lock up. And please, locking the drawer and leaving the key in the lock is not really securing it, is it?

Circulation staff can have a key to the drawer that they carry with them. Don't have a key at the front desk on a huge dowel rod marked "CASH DRAWER" or "REGISTER". I'd laugh along with you, but I've actually seen that one so much it's depressing!

3. Keep library keys with you at all times and don't leave them lying around. Put them on one of those little coil gizmos that fit around your wrist or on a lanyard. Belt clips are also perfect for the male staff. If you have so many keys that they weigh you down to carry them, it is way past the time to re-key the building.

4. Be very careful in handling your deposits. There is no such thing as a night deposit. Always take money to the bank during regular business hours. Break up the times you go as best you can. Don't always go, for example, every Tuesday and Thursday at high noon.

I'll never forget what I saw during a visit to the Midwest, when arriving at a library with my host. We saw the branch manager going across the lot with a bank bag with the bank's name clearly marked on the side. He waved at us with the bag and shouted from across the lot, "I didn't know you guys would be here so soon. I always go to the bank about one o'clock."

5. Never leave your pocketbook or briefcase where it can be seen by patrons. I know this can be inconvenient at times, but if you are ever ripped off it makes for a dangerous environment because the thief now thinks your library is an easy mark and he *will* return. And if you, a fellow employee or a patron catch him in the act, he could assault someone. Always secure these items.

6. Staff areas should be locked at all times. Staff areas should be locked at all times. Staff areas should be locked at all times. No, this is not a misprint. Staff areas should be locked at all times. You never want to walk into back rooms or offices and find someone who is not supposed to be there.

7. Double check all bathrooms, stacks, study rooms and the rest of the public areas to make sure all patrons are out before you close. You do not want to be alone with some unknown individual after closing. If you think that you might have trouble with someone at closing, call the police well before you start closing procedures so you won't be by yourself with the potential problem.

8. Never let anyone other than authorized library staff or service contractors into the building before

opening or after you closed. If you haven't been advised that Billy Bob's carpet cleaning is coming, don't let them in. The same goes for the telephone guy here to "check the phone lines." He had better have some ID and you had better ask him for it.

9. Follow your nature-given intuition. If you sense something is not right, call the police or your security. Meet with the local police in your town or district and show them you have security procedures in place and that your staff is trained. Impress upon the officers that you will not call unless you really need them, so that when they do get the call, they will prioritize it. Having a good relationship with them will also come in handy if you ever have bad police response. You'll already know someone in charge to help correct the problem.

10. If you are working alone in the branch (and that is one of the most dangerous things you can do, and you can quote me), keep your phone use and duties to an absolute minimum. The standard rule is: *the less staff that is on hand, the more your awareness goes up.* Never admit to being alone to a patron you don't really know. If a patron asks you if you are by yourself, say something like, "No, Jeff is in the back, but he's also busy. One of us will be with you in a moment." While the patron's inquiry is usually an innocent one, there is no point in exposing your vulnerability.

These ten points are the main things you need to consider. I would bet that you recognize something in this list that you can change. Let me just warn you that old habits die hard, and most employees are often negative about changing their ways, even if it is for their own safety. And of the staff that is already safety minded, there are even fewer who will readily go along with new procedures if they are seemingly inconvenient to them. But as the saying goes, "the only thing that doesn't change is change," so it's part of their job to adapt and help make the workplace safer for everyone.

Chapter Seven:
A Strategy for Basic Documentation

I've seen all kinds of security report forms in my career. For some reason a lot of people think the more complicated they are the more effective they are. What lengthy forms actually usually do is raise your sense of anxiety over being involved in an incident, thus having to be a part of the report process. The forms are so complicated, staff will do anything to avoid them and that includes ignoring situations that need to be documented.

I've included a form at the end of this chapter that is quite simple and multi-functional to help you. Let me explain and walk you through it. It's not the only form that you will eventually need, but it is a vital start.

At the beginning of each day, you start off with a new log. At the top you see there are several headings. "Type" will be filled in with either an "*" or one of the incident types (which are listed at the bottom of the sheet). The "#" symbol column will be used for assigning the incident a number. "Time" is simply the time whatever you are notating took place. The Staff and Police/Medic columns are filled in with the person who first responded to or noticed the situation. Other staff involved are added in the narrative.

Ok, so let's say a group of teenagers have food and beverages over in the library business section. You tell them that it's not allowed and they comply by taking it all outside to finish. On your log you would put an "*" under "Type" to denote a *rule advisement*, the time, the staff member involved and then just write in what happened to the right of the form. For example: "Advised four teenagers they could not eat in the library."

Now let's say that this group gave you a hard time and refused to dispose of their food. You made your best effort to communicate with them, but nothing worked and you decide they have to leave for the day, so you eject them. This would now be a *security incident*, not just a *rule advisement*. On the log you would Type it as a "MR" for "Miscellaneous Rule Infraction" (look again at your choices for incident types). You would write in the time and the staff who ejected them. You would write the narrative as something similar to, "Group of teenagers, advised no food allowed, but refused to comply. I warned them that if they did not dispose of the food, they would have to leave for the day. They chose to leave."

If you know their names they could be added to your report. The whole incident narrative is written on the log taking up ever how many lines necessary. So you are combining notations for every time you advise someone of rule infractions (which helps document to administration how busy you are with controlling the library environment), with actual security incidents.

Assigning the incident number in the # column is very simple. On your computer, make a log of your incidents as they occur. Give each one a six digit number. Make the first two digits the year like so: 06-0001. The next one will be 06-0002 and so forth.

And while you are making a log on your PC, be sure to make another list of the names of people you ban for easy reference, as well as the date and length of the ban. Cross reference it with your incident number so you can easily go back to the respective daily security log if you need the details of the incident. Now you can look up the banned patrons by name instead of first going through all the incident logs.

Another use of the form is to make notes regarding suspicious behavior. Among the listing at the bottom of the sheet I have a "PPL" for "Potential Problem Log Entry." Let's say you have some fellow that comes in and sits at a table with a magazine. You notice that he never really looks at the reading material even though he is turning the pages. He is too busy looking around the building or maybe staring at one of the staff or one of the patrons. Your instincts tell you that staff may have to address his actions with him at some point, but he hasn't really stepped over that line yet. This is a perfect situation for the "PPL" entry.

Go back to your daily Security Log. Under "Type" write in "PPL" and note the time and staff member involved. Then you would proceed to just write in a narrative of what you observed. This is for future reference if you ever need to talk to him or possibly eject him from the library. It just gives you more justification for action you possibly might have to take. Describe him as best you can and of course note his name if you have it. I sometimes use a moniker if I don't have a name, but remember to keep it professional and not prejudicial or demeaning. There is a big difference in referring to an unknown behavior problem as "Magazine Man" rather than "Dirty Old Bastard #2"!

Now we have another incident. A man is obviously very intoxicated and trying to ask everyone for money. You call your security or the police. When they arrive they obtain his name and inform him of his ban. On your security log you would enter "AD" under the type for alcohol/drugs. Then list the time and initial staff and responding officer. You would then proceed to write up the *who, what, when, and where* in the descriptive column, again using as many lines as you need.

Keep in mind that your security log may become a court document so print or write neatly and only use black ink. Keep the narrative brief and professional. I prefer a hand written log so I can move around with it on a clip board if necessary, but you could of course put this on a computer and use it that way.

If the police or medic ever has to be called note their names in the column provided. When a *situation* officially becomes an *incident* is up to you, but when you call the police or medic to help that is always an incident.

Of course, this is a sample form and when you create your own, you can make columns and spaces as large as you like. Store them or scan them into a computer for posterity. I still have my first library report from June of 1989. You never know when you may need them for some type of court proceeding.

SECURITY LOG

Day: _____ Date: _____

Type	#	Time	Staff	Police/ Medic	Narrative

Types:

A – Assault

TH – Theft

SOL – Soliciting

PI – Patron Injury

AD – Alcohol/Drugs

TR – Trespass

BT – Bomb Threat

MR – Misc. Rule Infraction

DC – Disorderly Conduct

OT – Other

DTP – Damage to Property

PPL – Potential Problem Log Entry

CM – Computer Misuse

FA – Fire Alarm

EI – Employee Injury

* – Rule Advisement

In Closing

I hope I've helped you with some practical advice that you can return to your library and use *today*. I would just like to leave you with another thought.

As you can tell from the content of the book, I gleaned a great deal of guidance from my martial art days. One instructor sat me down after a class one evening and drew a circle on a piece of paper. In the middle of the circle, he marked a large dot. "The circle is a hurricane," he explained, "and the dot is the eye of the storm, where everything is calm and serene. In your life, Warren, you need to fight your way through the calamity of the harsh winds to get to the eye and stay there as best you can. As I see you, I think you are always in the storm." He was right. Of course, my 16 year old mind could only process this in a literal way and I had a long way to go before I could actually understand and do what he suggested, but I never forgot it.

Switch now to years later, when hurricane Hugo came slugging up through South and North Carolina. In Charlotte, I sat through a very long night in my living room as 98 mile an hour winds pounded the front of my house. At one point, the storm stopped and I went outside to take a look. I found out later this was at a point when the hurricane's eye was in my area. Everything was completely still and silent. So help me, I immediately thought about what my old instructor was trying to tell me so many years ago.

We all work through the storms of our life attempting to find a little happiness and contentment. Our jobs, both in working with the public and with our co-workers, can be the source of great trials and challenges in our life. I finally understood and found the "eye," and I worked hard to get there. I struggle within myself periodically to stay there. Today, as I unlock the library front door, I'll remind myself not to let circumstances at work push me back into the chaos of the storm. What about you?

About the Author

Warren Graham is a nationally renowned security, safety and customer service consultant recognized for his unique approach to personal and professional safety. His experiences include 25 years as a security professional, nine years as a retail manager and 35 years as a martial artist with teaching credentials in five disciplines.

Since 1989 Warren has served as Security and Safety Manager for the Public Library of Charlotte and Mecklenburg County, developing and overseeing its security procedures. His on the job experiences give him a unique perspective on the problems front-line library staff encounter on a daily basis.

Over the past decade, Warren has traveled the nation, training thousands of librarians to effectively control their work environment. His engaging, interactive training sessions have earned him recognition as the "guru" of library security.